Where is Lucy?

A beautiful day at the park turns into 14 days that we will never forget.

Where is Lucy?
Copyright © 2009 by Sharon Crooks

All rights reserved. No part of this book may be reproduced in any form or by any electronic or mechanical means including storage and retrieval systems without permission in writing from Sharon Crooks

ISBN-13: 9781605000329

Printed in the United States of America
Powered by Bookemon. www.bookemon.com

A special thank you to my dear friend Teresa Cooney who suggested I write a childrens story about Lucy and Bailey.

Also, thank you to my sister Bayla McDougal for her encouragement, and her daughter Jenny McDougal for her guidance.

We want to thank everyone for their thoughts and prayers during those 14 days.

This is a true story.

Front cover drawing by Bayla McDougal
Photos by Scott Crooks
Back cover drawing by Paul Crooks

This is Lucy. She lives with her sister Bailey and her family, Paul and Sharon. This is her baby picture.

This is Bailey. She lives with her sister Lucy and the family. This is her baby picture.

They like to play together with their toys.

When they were puppies they learned to go on walks with their new collars and leashes. Going for walks was a special time with the family.

After a walk they would get a treat and play some more.

Then they would sleep.

Shhhh....

Lucy and her sister Bailey loved to run around in their big back yard. They would chase birds, squirrels, and of course each other. They would run up and down the fence barking and playing with the neighbor's dogs.

They always have fun.

They were always together. When they were done playing, they would curl up with each other and take a nap. This was one of their favorite things.

These two dogs loved to go for long walks with their family. Everyday they would get their leashes on and away they would go. It was fun to walk around the neighborhood, the school across the street and the park. They saw the same familiar things; kids riding their bikes, people walking their dogs and children playing.

When they got home, they would curl up and relax.

One day, Paul and Sharon decided to take them to a big, beautiful park to let them run. As soon as Lucy and Bailey jumped out of the car, they saw things they had never seen before. They saw great big trees and tall prairie grass that towered over their heads.

The sky was perfect with only a few clouds. It smelled of sweet flowers and fresh cut grass on a warm summer morning. Lucy and Bailey walked and ran around and played for a long time.

They were having lots of fun.

It was nearing time to leave when all of a sudden, a rabbit jumped in front of Lucy. She barked and barked and chased after it. Bailey followed her. Paul and Sharon could hear them barking way off in the distance.

Just like that, they were gone.........

Paul and Sharon called and whistled for them over and over, but Lucy and Bailey could not hear them because they were barking so loudly. For a very long time they searched for their dogs, but neither Lucy or Bailey came back.

Had they run away?

Finally, after many hours, Bailey found her way back to the car, but Lucy was not with her. Bailey was tired and very thirsty but most of all she was sad because Lucy was missing.

What had happened? These two dogs were always together. Did Lucy find a new friend, or maybe she just wanted to run and play some more. Maybe she got lost.

For many days and nights, Paul and Sharon and their friends searched for Lucy. They drove up and down gravel roads and walked all around the park calling for her, but she was no where to be found.

They put signs around the park about their lost black and white dog with their phone number on it hoping someone would call.

LOST!

Small Dog - 25 lbs.

Black and White

Beagle/Basset mix

Name - Lucy

Call: 555-555-5555

Reward!

Maybe Lucy had wandered off to the pond. She had never been to a pond before. There were farms with cows and chickens out near the park. She had never seen those either. Maybe that was where she had gone.

Back at home, Bailey was sad. Her best friend and sister was missing.

She had to walk by herself.

She had to sleep by herself.

She was very lonely.

Bailey missed Lucy a lot. She would walk around the back yard looking for her, but she was not there.

She would look out the front window hoping to see her sister but she was not there either.

For several days it rained and stormed. Paul and Sharon were very worried about Lucy. They were sad knowing that she was all alone out there somewhere.

They spent many hours, day and night, looking for her but they could not find her.

Then one day the phone rang. It was a man who had seen a black and white dog like Lucy. Paul and Sharon drove out near the park. They called and whistled for her, but she did not come.

It had been 12 days. Where could Lucy be? Was she okay? Was she scared? Was she hurt? Why didn't she come when she was called?

The family missed her very much.

The next day, a lady called. She had seen a dog that looked like Lucy wandering around in a field. The family drove out and called for her: LUCY! LUCY! but they did not hear a sound. Lucy was not there either.

Bailey did not have any one to play with. It sure was boring and quiet without Lucy.

Finally, the next day they got another phone call from a farmer that had found a dog in his barn. It had been 14 days, could it really be Lucy!!!

Paul and Sharon drove to the barn as fast as they could. When they got to the barn, there was Lucy!

She was so excited to see them that she wiggled and wiggled and gave them lots of wet kisses.

They were very happy to see her!

Lucy was thirsty, hungry and very dirty. She had some bug bites and cuts.

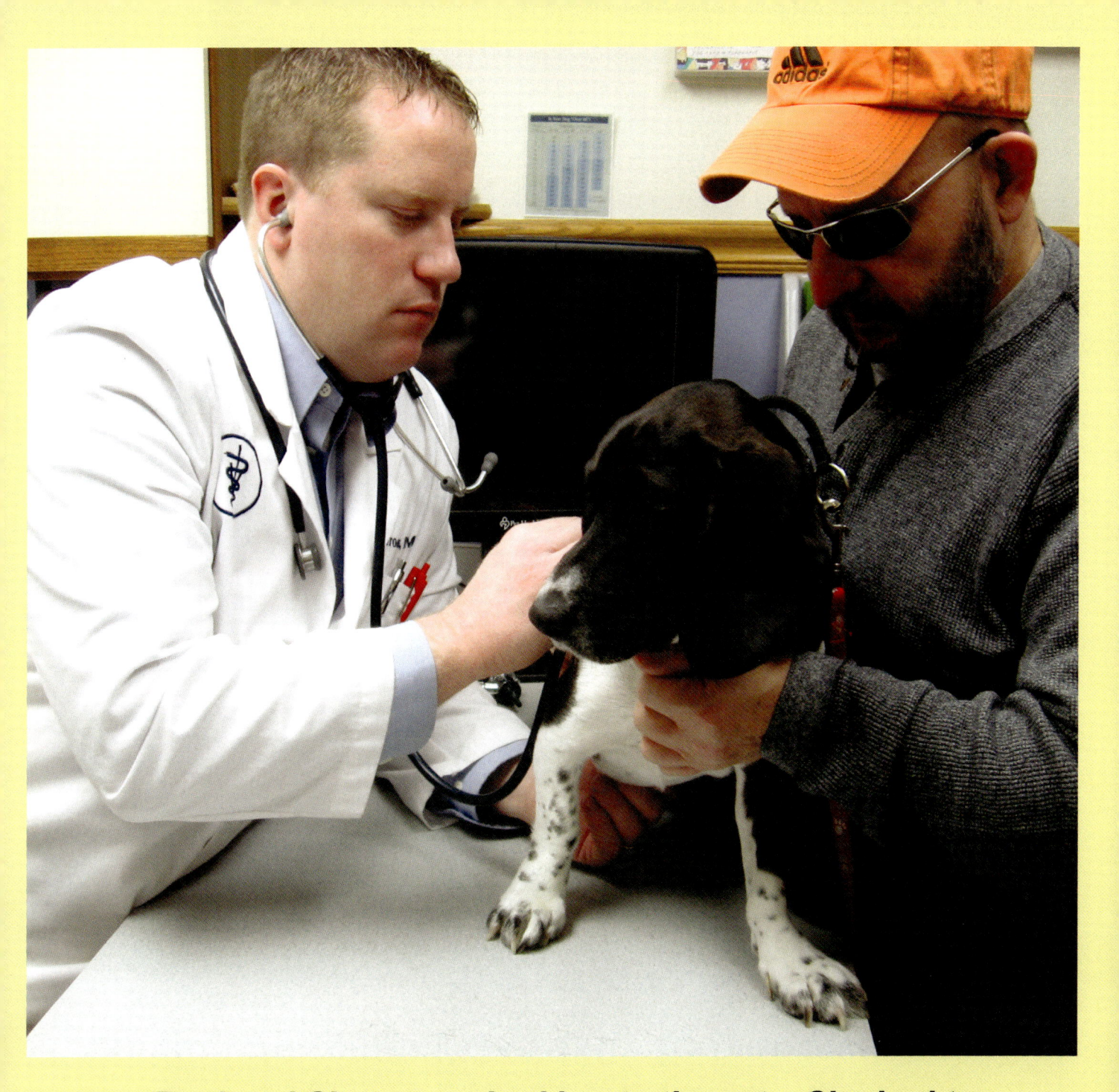

Paul and Sharon rushed her to the vet. She had to stay at the vet for a few days to make sure she was OK. The Doctor said she was in good condition for being on her own for 14 days and that she really took care of herself. Lucy is a strong dog and a lucky dog.

Finally she got to come home. We were all so glad to have her back!!!

When Lucy got home, Bailey was so excited to see her! Finally, they were together again!

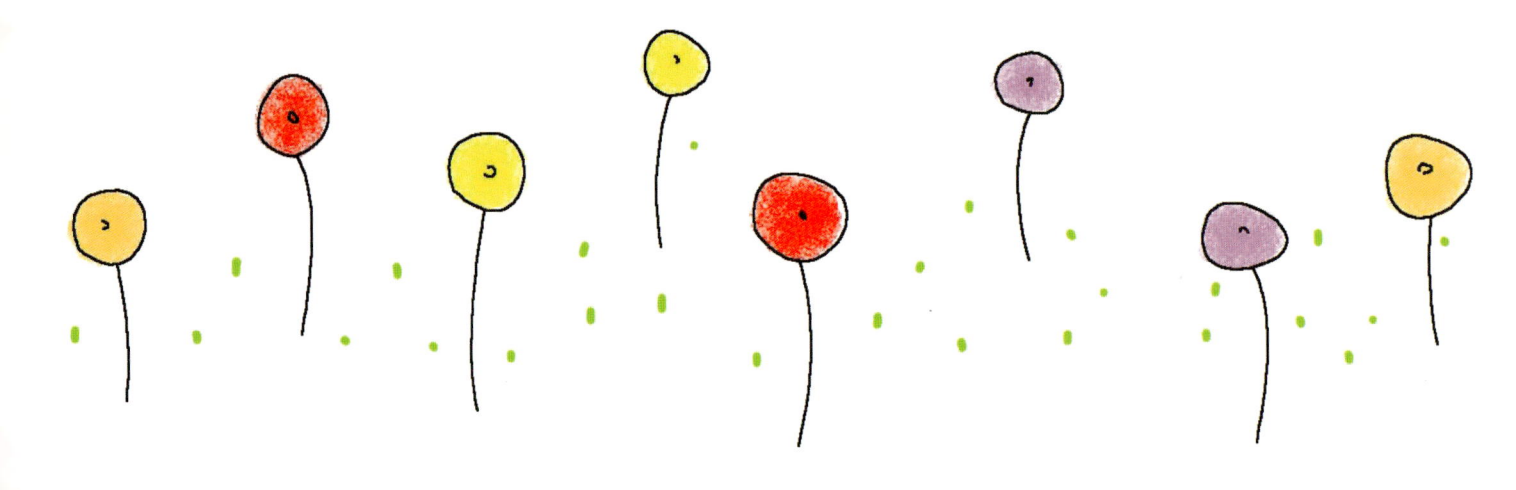

They ran round and round the yard barking at the birds, squirrels and the neighbor's dog. They were very happy! Finally, they did their most favorite thing, they took a nap together just like old times, never to be apart again.

I LOVE MY SISTER

THE END

Printed in the United States